Guide to Writing

Job-Winning

Resumes

Ella A. Williams

Dedication

This book is dedicated to my children Sandra, Maxine,
Elaine and Paul,
who have shared their hearts in applauding
and inspiring me to
accomplish this very important milestone.

Contents

Acknowledgement

On this rocky journey to success, first and foremost, I want to give God thanks for the legacy of His wisdom that has enabled me thus far. And, even when I am scared, I believe and proceed according to His Words from Psalm 32:8: *I will instruct you and teach you the way that you must go; I will guide you with my eyes.* Thank you, dear Heavenly Father. Your perfect will be done.

In hindsight, and without prejudice, I want to give a big shout-out to my son Paul who, for as long as I can remember, has been and continue to be one of my very first and strongest motivators in writing this book. Over time, he has endorsed me mentally, physically and financially, always keeping me up-to-date with the latest technology that has enabled me to work stress-free. Paul, thanks-a-million for your wisdom, love, and confidence! You are indeed an exceptional son.

Special mention also to my daughter, Elaine, for the selfless, ongoing support you offer in love and deed always. Thank you, my princess, for giving me the assurance and inspiration each day that I am your 'queen.' And, to my daughters, Sandra and Maxine, thanks for your prayers, support and care throughout the ages and tough times. You never let me forget that God is my refuge and strength, and how very proud you are of 'Mother.' And to my grandson, Kurt Jr., for the "stellar artwork" you performed on the book cover. Thanks for your selfless contribution. Feeling so blessed and thankful to God for the priceless gifts you all are, my precious children, and immediate families. It is often said, time is the healer, so here I am son, daughters, grand and great-grandchildren, nieces, close families, and special friends, I finally finished the book! Thanks for all your encouragement and support. Most importantly, thanks for believing in me and cheering me on to accomplish this long-awaited dream of writing a book.

Last, but not least, I give thanks to Coach Shelly, my mentor—and a true advocate. Dr. Shelly Cameron, Author, Speaker, Career and Motivational Coach, you have earned my highest and most profound appreciation. You are a genius in your craft. Thank you for the great diplomacy you developed and implemented to motivate me when I encountered a standstill or, realistically, had a mental block. Thanks for coaching me with such humility, grace and Christian kindness every step of the way. With deep gratitude to Almighty God for His divine appointment, I feel especially blessed to have crossed paths with you.

"Everything you fought for was not for yourself but for those who come after you."

Chadwick A. Boseman

Foreword

Ella A. Williams, a visionaire was walking around with a dream. A book publishing dream to make the lives of people she encountered better as they embarked on their career journey. In pursuit of this dream, her paths crossed with the Ralph Hogges and Benjamin Cowins Writers Group of South Florida. A group spiritually designed to build the lives of writers of color—confident, she walked in. This newbie was on the agenda to present her expertise.

Presentation over, I was divinely led to sit with her writing genre. We got talking and discussed our background and mutual experiences. I shared about my book *"GreenLight: When God Says Go."* It was not a practice of mine to share that so early in an exchange, but I did, then walked away. Apparently, the Holy Spirit intervened and Miss Ella—as I call her, found the answer she was looking for. God had told her to 'Go,' but she was fearful. A fear that is so common to us all when we step into new territory.

Through divine intervention, I immediately vowed to guide her to achieve that predestined plan. A dream that intercepts with others to accomplish a purpose that would last beyond her lifetime and one that would be treasured by her inner circle. A dream to help others find their true potential through the first step into a new or changed career.

Ella is the consummate businesswoman. She captured the award for recognition in the Library of Congress National Register's "Who's Who in Executives and Professionals" through her business affiliation in South Florida. This spliced with her publication in the Miami Herald's Careers and Workplace newspaper.

Armed with this outstanding accomplishment, who else should write this guide than a woman who has the experience, know-how, and one who cares about the lives of others? None other than this woman of God who has been a writer for more than two decades.

Ella's specialized training in Communication enabled her to take readers through the job application process using this book, Guide to Writing Job-Winning Resumes. She leads readers through the evolution of careers, how-to-write resumes, and the different types of letters that readers interface with throughout their job search journey.

If you are on the hunt for a new job opportunity, get your copy of this short informative guide. Allow it to lead you to accomplish your divinely led career goal as this book writing process did for Ella A. Williams.

--Dr Shelly Cameron

Organizational Development/HR Practitioner,
Author & Coach

Introduction

A Guide to Writing Job-Winning Resume is primarily created to inspire and educate future generations on the pros and cons of creating and writing their own *job-winning resumes and cover letter*s. The overall content of this book is based solely on the author's personal experience in drafting and writing job-winning/high impact resumes and/or cover letters from the scratch to finish. This easy, step-by-step guide is designed to teach you how to use ordinary, everyday action verbs in constructing meaningful sentences that convey the target message. Remember, the goal is to get noticed and ultimately land that dream job! This book is further intended to acquaint you with practical details and strategies required to build masterpiece resumes and/or cover letters that will *mesmerize* even the most finicky human resource/hiring critic. Note: Winning Resumes and Cover Letters do stand out—and yes, you do get noticed.

A Resume is that pivotal piece of the puzzle that often stands between one's success and failure in acing that dream job. While a resume is the highlight for job seekers, it can also be a challenge for the preparer. In today's rapidly expanding, fast-paced, social media era, a candidate's ultimate dream is to land the 'perfect' job from the classroom to the workforce. Frankly, some resumes (and cover letters) are usually human resources' worst nightmares and a detriment to the prospective employee. Sad to say, but many of these resumes and/or cover letters never make it to the opportunity pile; rather, they are tossed in the trash bin.

This brings us to the big question: ***What is a Resume?*** Resumes are essentially a dialogue between the employer and employee. A resume is the first point of contact between two parties; hence, it is imperative that your resume make a good, first impression. From both sides of the spectrum—applicants and employers alike—job hunting can be very stressful. While the employee's goal is to land that dream job, the employer, on the other hand, is focused on screening the best candidate for the job. Because it is customary for one job posting to attract numerous candidates at any given time, it makes job hunting more fiercely competitive. In this case, the "best" resume may win!

Frankly, I believe a resume should be everything but confusing, especially when candidates are honest about what they bring to the table. However, it never fails; employers, office managers and human resource managers—everywhere—never fail to make both selection and interview processes a job within itself. This can be gruelling or very depressing for the applicant. Understandably, I trust that this informative little book will serve as the catalyst in diminishing this type of intimidation and enable you to capitalize on the confidence to write your own effective job-winning resume and/or cover letter. After all, let's be realistic— the motto is, *doing it right the first time!*

Whether it is writing job-winning resumes and cover letters or similar correspondence—this little guide will be useful in many other spheres of correspondence. As well, it can also be used as a training tool in the development of proper sentence structure as it relates to grammar, punctuation, avoiding 'run-on' sentences, and using verbs, nouns, pronouns, adjectives, tenses and markings appropriately. A word of caution: It is imperative that you avoid typos—make good use of computer spellcheck and thesaurus (to interchange words), and insert symbols for proper formatting and easy reading. Later in this book, you will find great examples of *winning resumes and cover letters* that have contributed in building successful careers for generations before you.

Destined to write a book—just did not know when and how. For as long as I can remember, I received motivations from several families, friends and even strangers, including my nail technician. These people all benefited from my work, and has cheered me on to writing a book—some more explicit than others. In 2012, I stopped in at the nail shop for a routine manicure/pedicure where a casual conversation went like this: "*So, Ms. Ella, when are you going to write that book telling people how to write effective job-winning Resumes? Ms. Ella, I recommend that you go into fasting and prayer for 7-days and ask God what direction you are to take. But, it's time you write that book, and I will buy the first copy!*" Humbled and excited at the same time, I began jotting down notes, none of which came to fruition.

Although pursuing my childhood dream to write a book—any book—was still very much alive; the action remained dormant for years. It took me a lifetime to realize that there is a set time for everything under heaven. Now, eight years later, I received another *surreal* encounter which eventually led to the actual writing of this book. This was nothing short of a miracle! I am convinced that God is the only author and finisher of that faith that is the substance of things hoped for and the evidence of things not seen—but must be done. Impossible, I thought, but I did it; I wrote a book, and so you can. Follow your dreams and let a *guide to writing job-winning resumes* coach you along.

Finally, may this guidebook be a phenomenal blessing to those whose lives it will touch. Thank you for reading! It will make a great contribution and gift to the younger generation. Check it out and pick up a copy for your library or a friend.

SECTION ONE

THE MERGING OF
CAREERS & RESUMES

In a lifetime, we are born, we grow, we overcome, we achieve. Whether you are young, middle-aged, or old, Black, White, Caucasian or other, a career is inevitable. At some point in everyone's life, a career is mandatory. Careers are the hallmark to earning financial independence for one's lifetime. Whichever medium one chooses in making a future, be it academics, entrepreneurial, professional, occupational or otherwise, this segment of life is defined as a career. And, instantaneously, Careers automatically merges with Resumes—they do go hand-in-hand—both topics are fully illustrated in this guide.

Definition of careers

A Career is an expression used to describe an individual's life journey which he or she derives through training, employment and/or other method of functions or talents for a lifetime. In today's social media era, there are wide ranges of educational, counselling, human resource management and online materials that are available to assist an individual in mastering his/her career. Oxford English Dictionary defines career as a person's course or progress through life or a distinct portion of life. Career is also expressed in other forms such as profession and/or occupation. Hence, a career is viewed as a progression of job-related or other relevant experiences pursued by the individual through employment, education or otherwise.

Career choices

In their new edition of Career Choices and Changes, best-selling authors <u>Mindy Bingham, Sandy Stryker</u> addresses the 21st-century workplaces' realities. Career Choices is a step-by-step workbook/journal format **designed** to help the reader discover the careers that will match their passions, lifestyle aspirations, skills, and aptitudes. *It introduces a process for career and lifestyle decision-making that can be used repeatedly, thereby empowering the reader to productively navigate through a lifetime of workplace and personal change. A verified purchaser gave this book a five-star review rating, in which was written: *"This book takes kids through the decision-making process of choosing their life's work, sets up a plan B, and helps them validate their goals by walking them through the steps to achieve their goals."* Comments: *"Great info for any 14-24 year old."*

Career types

According to Behling and others, an individual's decision to join a firm could depend upon three factors: objective factor theory, subjective factor theory, and critical contact theory. These theories presume that candidates have a free choice of employers and careers. However, in this rapidly expanding technological era, it is predicted that many individuals between the ages of 18 and 38 will likely hold more than 10 jobs in their lifetime.

Comparatively speaking, in the real world, there are various types of careers—some of which can be perceived as habit-forming, scheming careers. These types of careers often entail greed, dealing in drugs, stealing, criminal activities, etc. These career choices are detrimental and can eventually lead the individual(s) into a lifetime of crime. Careers of this nature should be avoided at all costs. In the Bible, we are reminded that *by the sweat of the brow, we shall eat bread/food* [Gen. 3:19]. This makes it crystal clear that whatever we do in the name of a career is not always easy work. Examples of some lucrative, but hard/dangerous, careers include construction, minefields, and building roads and bridges.

It is human nature, however, to question our own abilities when it comes to careers. Presumptively, at times, we wish we were like others in their respective careers. Despite the feeling, this author is of the belief that God created each and every individual with a unique career plan for that person's life. Inborn or acquired, a career can be anything you want it to be. Careers are important. It is the standard means by which everyone in the society will eventually acquire a comfortable lifestyle of wealth and fulfilment. As stated earlier, for some people, careers are inherent; for others, like this author, a career can take up to a lifetime to come to fruition. Regardless of time or age, there are millions of different honest career types upon which one can build a stable life foundation.

Career comes in all colors, shapes and sizes. Some renowned career categories in the professional, academic, political, business-management realm consist of law, medicine, healthcare, education, engineering, clergy, engineers, government, and the list goes on. Other careers could take the path of hairdressing, carpentry, builder/construction, real estate, welding, plumbing, financing, accounting, to working in sales and services across numerous trades.

Nonetheless, whether you sing, dance, speak, write, preach or tell jokes, writing *job-winning resumes* and *cover letters* are directly linked to all career paths and have become a requirement for all job seekers.

In the sections that follow, the author has provided a simple step-by-step guide (along with prepared samples) on how to write your best *job-winning resumes, curriculum vitae/cv, cover letters, thank you letters, resignation letters, references, etc.*, that will get you noticed and ultimately hired.

SECTION TWO

GUIDE TO WRITING JOB-WINNING RESUMES

What is a Resume?

A Resume **is** that essential piece of the puzzle—it can be your enemy or your friend in landing or losing that dream job. Webster Dictionary defines *Resume* as a verb— an action verb—that means to ***start over, start again, carry on, continue, or pick-up where you left off.*** However, based on experience, a *Resume* is a document that simply serves as a dialogue between the employer and potential employee. Essentially, resumes are prerequisites and the invisible presence of the candidate on paper. It is the first point of contact between two parties, and the magnet that generates communication between these parties. It is customary that one job posting can attract masses of applicants; thus, making the job search more fiercely competitive. So, when it comes to writing resumes, always strive to make it a "winner."

Note*: Job-winning resumes* usually contain eye-catching phrases that start with strong action verbs, paying close attention to tenses (past and present) and proper sentence structuring for clarity and completion.

How long should my Resume be?

Taking into consideration the number of applicants vying for the same position in a single job posting, a one-to-two-page resume is highly recommended. With the use of today's social media, resumes are now being scanned for keywords; so, the shorter, the better your chance is of getting noticed. A well-written one-page resume, with work experience ranging up to 10 years (depending on one's age) is acceptable and could easily capture the interest of employers or hiring managers on the spot.

Why do we need Resumes?

Primarily, to find a job! Equally, the applicant's goal is basically to land that perfect job—the employer's goal is to choose that perfect candidate; it is that simple. On the contrary, looking from both sides of the spectrum—applicants and employers alike—job hunting can be a win or lose situation. For this reason, one should not settle for just a resume but always thrive to produce a "*job-winning*" *resume*—one that makes an excellent first impression that triggers a response to move the applicant from the stockpile to the interview process.

While a *resume* is the primary motivating factor for getting the job, it can also be very challenging for the preparer. In today's rapidly-expanding, fast-paced, social media era, a candidate's ultimate dream is to get the job. Nonetheless, let's be realistic, some resumes (and cover letters) are usually employers, human resources or hiring managers' worst nightmares, and a waste of time for the prospective employee. The raw truth is, quite often, many of these resumes and cover letters are dream-killers—and never made it past the trash bin.

Today, resumes and cover letters are no longer read; rather, they are scanned electronically for key words. Hence, at a glance, hiring managers now have the competitive edge of accepting or rejecting a resume on the spot. While this is not mandatory, most employers or organizations are especially intrigued when the applicant takes the initiative to learn about their company or operations. This action often helps to deepen the candidate's chance for consideration.

Frankly, this author believes resumes should be everything but complicated; however, it never fails. Employers, office managers and human resource managers—everywhere—always seem to make both the selection and interview process a real challenge. For some, this can be a nightmare that leaves a prospective employee in a state of panic. Understandably, this informative little book was designed to diminish this type of intimidation and capitalize on writing your own "*job-winning*" resume and cover letter with confidence. After all, you [too] can be a winner by doing it right the first time. Take advantage of this powerful *Guide to Writing Job-Winning Resumes*, authored by Ella Williams. Pick up a copy for yourself or give a gift to a loved one or friend.

Types of Resume Formats

Various articles describe the four most commonly used types of Resume formats as:

1. Reverse Chronological

2. Functional

3. Combination

4. Targeted, and a

   Fifth format, known as CV (Curriculum Vitae)

Reverse Chronological Resume

The reverse chronological Resume is considered the number one most universal format today. It is a structured format that most candidates use to feature job history or work experience in chronological order (starting with their most current and working backwards to the past—up to 10 years), which most employers accept. This format enables the reader to quickly scan work history, glance for potential gaps in employment, and visualize major accomplishments that would give the applicant an edge for consideration over his/her opponent. [Sample included.]

- **How do I know when to use a chronological resume format?**

  Suppose you maintain a record of continuous employment without significant gaps, and your experience is in harmony with the job you are applying for, then, by all means. In that case, the chronological format is easy and ideal for you.

Functional Resume

Slightly different from the reverse chronological mentioned above, the functional resume format focuses on the candidate's marketable skills and then targeted accomplishments. The entire profile of this format is focused on highlighting abilities that closely matches the job requirements listed. Those skills are placed at the beginning of the resume under the caption: *Profile and/or Summary Qualifications*, using bullets and "action" verbs to clearly highlight the candidate's skill sets. Under work experience caption, accomplishments are preferred over actual job duties. [Sample included.]

- **How do I know when to use a functional resume format?**

  If you have lapses in employment, are in the middle of a career transition, or a recent college grad with limited work experience or have a diverse background with no clear career path, this is the most effective resume format to use.

Combination or Hybrid Resume

The combination or hybrid resume format is one that combines elements of both the reverse chronological and functional concept. This format is considered to be more detailed and represents information in a more concise manner, which can be easily viewed by recruiters.

Similar to the functional format, the hybrid/ combination resume often begins with a ***profile or summary of qualifications.*** This introductory section typically is a synopsis of the individual's strongest skills, along with any special achievements or recognition from prior positions that would be relevant to the position applied for. This format continues with a chronological listing of work experience, as well as educational background, additional training, professional affiliations, etc., are also applicable. [See sample.]

- **How do I know when to use a combination resume format?**

  This resume format is ideal if you want to detail work experience to show hiring managers the type of employee you are. A major downfall with this combination format is that it can often convey too much information that some employers view as being over-qualified. Hence, the combination format can be misconstrued at times. Nonetheless, if you decide to use this format—write with discretion!

Targeted Resume

Targeted resumes are customized in detail to accommodate a particular job posting. Everything from objective, qualifications to educational experience is focused around the job you applied for. A targeted resume is very time-consuming to build, as it is mostly based on qualifications rather than experience. As a result, careful consideration has to be placed into compiling information in order to avoid over-exaggeration.

- **How do I know when to use the targeted resume format?**

  Much like the combination format, target resumes have stark similarities. If you are a student with very little or no experience whatsoever, the target resume format will be perfect for you to build upon in selling more of your personal attributes and/or skills. [See sample.]

Curriculum Vitae

People often tend to confuse Resumes with Curriculum Vitae (CV); they compare them as one and the same. However, there are stark differences in the composition, style, appearance, and definitions of resumes and curriculum vitae.

Ella A. Williams

What is a CV or Curriculum Vitae?

The dictionary defines Curriculum Vitae as a Latin word for "course of life." Often shortened as CV or Vitae, it is used to chronicle a complete record of an individual's life/career, and can be extensive depending on that individual's accomplishments. Vitae can be plural (curricula vitae) or possessive. In contrast, Vitae is written quite differently from a Resume. Resumes are typically a brief 1–2-page summary of qualifications and work experience for employment purposes, and often is represented in highlighted format. In many countries (like the USA and Canada), a Resume is chosen for its brevity over a CV. The resume is typically the first point of contact between a potential employee and the employer. It is primarily used to screen the applicant and ultimately set up a job interview.

Vitae/CV, on the other hand, is often prepared citing all details related to candidates or high echelon career professionals including doctors, professors, teachers, attorneys, nurse practitioners, corporate executives, political, government type occupations, and those pursuing post-secondary programs, scholarships, grants and bursaries.

In the 21st century, it has become popular for applicants to provide an electronic text of their CV to

21

employers using email, an online employment website, or a job-oriented social-networking-service website. Hence, it is recommended that you include keywords that are relevant to the position applied for. Example: Billing Management or Accounts Receivable Management could be coupled with key action verbs like "forecast," "orchestrate," or "calculate." Strong, actionable keywords will jump out at recruiters or hiring managers and make your CV stand out.

How do I Write a Curriculum Vitae/CV

A Curriculum Vitae/CV generally starts with the candidate's academia background, followed by training/ certifications, etc., a synopsis of his/her work history (listing only company names, dates and tittles held), and ending with professional affiliations, other distinguished accolades and/or achievements, and references. Finally, if you must include an objective/summary, this caption can be placed at the very end of your Vitae/CV, above the caption "reference." Practically speaking, a Curriculum Vitae/CV can be short (1-3 pages) or long (anywhere from 5 to 25 pages), depending on the individual's professional and didactic accomplishments (including research, lectures, books, etc.). [See samples.]

Strengths/Weaknesses of Resume

Like everything else, this author believes writing *job-winning* resumes are basically a blend of art and science that gains momentum on accuracy, composition and presentation. Bottom-line, it is dependent upon the creativity and depiction of the artist. For best results, let's look at some pros and cons in the form of strengths and weaknesses.

Strengths

Prior to writing a *job-winning r*esume, it is imperative that you do your homework. Before sitting at your computer, you must first gather all relevant information that will help you eliminate the guesswork, confusion or exaggeration. Here are a few tips to follow:

- ✓ Make a resume checklist.

- ✓ Target your audience or employer of choice.

- ✓ Conduct research to learn history on the company's business operations to determine if this is the right job and place for you.

- ✓ When writing, use clear, concise expressions, emphasizing on spelling/grammar & punctuation.

- ✓ Differentiate resume from curriculum vitae/cv. (Curriculum vitae/CV could be short 1-5 pages) or (long up to 25 pages and more for academic/ research purposes.)

✓ Organize easy-to-read pages, symmetrically with balances between content and white space.

✓ Use standard fonts: Times New Roman, Arial, Century, etc., sizes 12, 11 (largest); 10 (smallest).

✓ Strategically incorporate keywords from the job description that closely matches your skills set.

✓ Embellish on accomplishments, if possible (e.g., sales or $ increase, # of people served, and/or objective or % achieved)

Example, instead of:

- Resolved customer service issues… you could use:

- Increased department sales by 30%, based on ongoing excellence in customer service support.

✓ Be truthful about who you are—performance reflects heavily on honesty.

✓ Be 'grammatically correct,' avoid run-on sentences and/or fabrications/fibs.

✓ Understand the importance of making a good, but lasting impression with your words.

✓ Opt for 'quality,' not 'quantity'—remember, more is not always better, in every case.

✓ Use strong action verbs to structure sentences and/or accomplishments. Below is a list of popular/modern 'action' verbs that can be used to compile and write bold statements:

Accelerated	Coordinated	Forfeited	Maximized
Accomplished	Conducted	Facilitated	Maintained
Achieved	Created	Formulated	Originated
Administrated	Compiled	Featured	Oversaw
Arranged	Developed	Implemented	Organized
Analyzed	Delegated	Instituted	Operated
Approved	Designed	Initiated	Orchestrated
Capitalized	Distinguished	Established	Coached/Trained

Weaknesses/Pitfalls

Please pay particular attention to these pitfalls, especially if you are an international applicant. Prior to writing your resume or curriculum vitae/cv, conduct your research and compile information with the following goals in mind:

✓ Avoid outlandish designs like including borders, capitals in the text, and bold/colorful fonts.

✓ Avoid the use of tables, if possible—it often overcrowds the resume and distorts presentation.

✓ Personal information should include legal name, address, and contact only.

(Birthdate, picture, height, country of origin, etc., are not generally required, unless requested).

✓ Stay clear of the use of pronouns—(first person such as *I did, I managed, I partnered*, etc.).

✓ Include only relevant information (that can be justified to an employer at the interview).

✓ Clarity and information flow are pivotal—employers only scan a Resume/CV for a few seconds.

✓ Avoid questionable gaps in work history; these can be fixed by explaining that you have been travelling or took a career hiatus to care for an elderly parent, etc.

✓ Spelling and grammatical errors—a "no-no"—unacceptable—and must be avoided by all possible means. (One sure way is to ask someone else to read over your Resume/CV or be modest, get a second opinion, accept criticism and make changes.

A note of caution: It is crucially important and strongly recommended to avoid typos, at all costs. Make good use of computer spellcheck and thesaurus tools; they are perfect pals in assisting with proper word usage, formatting and, most importantly, providing clarity for easy reading.

The Legacy of Books

*"As humans, we die, but books
live on forever, culturally and
intellectually enriching the lives
of future generations."*

--- Ralph Hogges

SECTION THREE

CAREER LETTERS

When it comes to finding a job, resumes and cover letters are considered the ultimate marketing tools. They are mandatory requirements that aid the individual in obtaining employment and/or a specific job. They are the silent marketers that convey the applicant's credentials to employers/human resources and/or hiring managers. Generally, a well-written resume can be submitted single-handedly; however, some employers/ hiring managers often request attachment of a cover letter with the resume.

There are at least three different types of letters associated with the topic of resume. The most important of them all is the cover letter. However, along your career path, it is considered a courtesy for one to produce a thank-you letter, and occasionally, you may have to write a resignation letter.

What is a Cover Letter?

You asked: A cover letter is another medium used to market the candidate applying for the job. While it is not always mandatory, cover letters usually accompany resumes at the request of the employer; it functions as a more personal introduction that highlights the applicant's interest, qualifications, and availability for the job. The cover letter's 2nd paragraph basically consists of an overview of professional status (including academic, work experience or related skills), and ends with the individual vying for an interview. A cover letter is usually one page in length and focuses primarily on the position applied for.

What is a Thank-you Letter?

A thank you letter serves basically as a courtesy, thanking the human resource or hiring manager for the opportunity to interview. Today, thank-you letters can be sent (via email) up to three days after the interview or prior to receiving the job offer. The thank you letter should be short, insightful, and on the point.

What is a Resignation Letter?

From time to time, people face the challenge of writing a resignation letter. This is also a very simplified letter and one that is presented when an employee decides to leave his/her current job for whatever reason. The resignation letter is two-fold: it makes for a smoother transition and is legally binding for both parties.

Therefore, whether writing job-winning resumes, cover letters or other correspondence, this book is designed to guide you in developing and writing more effectively. It aids in proper sentence structuring, grammar/spelling and punctuation, avoiding use of 'run-on' sentences/phrases and pronouns, use of bullets, action verbs, and proper tenses (past and present).

You can review samples of job-winning resumes, cover letters, thank you letter, and resignation letter later in this guide or for further assistance, you can email us at smeinc@hotmail.com

SECTION FOUR

OVERALL SUMMARY

Recapping earlier, this little guide's primary purpose is to aid amateur resume preparers in building effective *job-winning* resumes/cover letters. Additionally, it is also designed as a didactic tool to edify young and old alike in maximizing the use of action verbs and punctuation usage and eliminating the use of pronouns, run-on sentences and phrases, such as the "first-person" stigma. For best results, the inexperienced writer could start framing his/her resume by asking the following five questions:

- WHO am I?

- WHY do I want this job?

- WHAT can I do for this company?

- WHERE do I see myself in five years?

- HOW do I plan to get there?

Once you are able to honestly answer these questions, half your job is done!

Resume Formatting Tips

While most resume writers comfortably follow a chronological or functional format, it is often said that the chronological style is more commonly used. However, new graduates, career changers and people re-entering the job market may benefit more from using the functional format. Variations are; a chronological resume highlights work history and past career accomplishments, while a functional resume highlights your abilities and educational achievements. Whatever format you decide to use, it is imperative that you review, edit, spellcheck and read over your resume for clarity and completeness.

Header

The resume header should contain clear, concise information about the applicant, consisting of

- Complete legal name
- Complete mailing address
- Telephone and/or cellphone numbers
- Email address

Body of the Resume

Immediately following your personal information is an "Objective." However, in today's resumes, ***training and*** *coaching professionals recommend the use of a summary of qualifications or professional profile as opposed to an "objective."* Creating a perfect objective, at times, presents many difficulties. However, a **professional profile and/or summary of qualifications section** generally conveys a synopsis of your strongest and most productive skills, listed in eye-catching phrases, using bullets.

BASIC HEADINGS APPEARING IN A RESUME ARE AS FOLLOWS:

OBJECTIVE or CAREER FOCUS

The word Objective is an old axiom that is optional or, in some cases, obsolete on today's Resumes. An objective can be somewhat complex to write. Its main disadvantage is limiting the candidate's potential in position choices.

However, if you are required to write an Objective (preferably, Career Focus) you will concentrate on 'what can I do for this company'; hence your statement would be generic and could read:

To coordinate resources, build relations, and achieve the bottom-line objective in a growth-orient organization. or

To make growth contributions in an organization that thrives on experience, commitment and teamwork.

Following Career Focus is

PROFILE or SUMMARY OF QUALIFICATIONS

This section is a synopsis of your strongest skills, could contain an overview followed by core strengths in a listing of bullets, as follows:

PROFESSIONAL PROFILE

MSN/BSN/RN Certified professional Nurse Educator/ Administrator and Adult-Gerontology Primary Care Nurse Practitioner with remarkable interpersonal and people skills. Demonstrated supervisory and case management capabilities to build relations and achieve organizational objectives. More than 20 years recurring experience in, but not limited to, hospital, nursing home, primary care, and students' facilitator roles. In-depth knowledge in Medicare/ Medicaid and OSHA guidelines as it relates to working with state agencies, delivering ultimate patient care, and documentation proficiency.

Core strengths:

- Caregiver in *ICU/CCU, Hospice, Telemetry, Med/Surg, Psychiatry/Mental Health and Community Nursing*.

- Objective-driven team leader with ability to communicate at-ease in management and staff-level meetings.

- Ability to triage, counsel, support and care for individuals in crisis and/or emergency situations.

- Five years teaching nursing education at Associate and Bachelor's degree levels.

- Adjunct Faculty at Nova Southeastern University, Florida National University, and Miami-Dade College.

- Familiar with proper use and application of modern computerized medical instrumentations including Epics, and system software of Amisys.

TECHNICAL SKILLS/PERSONAL ATTRIBUTES

Could include language proficiency (if any), computer and other technological knowledge or expertise and use of contemporary office systems/machinery, which are job-related.

Ella A. Williams

EXPERIENCE or EMPLOYMENT HISTORY

Listing your jobs in chronological order–from most current first with company name, job title, date/duration of position and duties performed.

Note: In today's job market, future employers are more interested in "accomplishments" than "job duties." As a result, your resume will have more merit showing statistical values, such as:

- *Organized & purged computerized data, gradually improving production by 50%*

- *Increased development program resources by 20% in the first quarter of the fiscal year*

- *Boosted semi-annual sales between 25% & 30%, which compounded annual growth*

- *Negotiated & maintained 100% recurring business across geographical lines*

- *Managed full P&L operations, showing consistent profits goals in excess of 100%*

EDUCATION

In the event you are writing a Curriculum Vitae/CV, instead of a Resume, your education should also appear in chronological order, starting at the very beginning of the Vitae, followed by your personal information. On a Resume, education can be placed at the beginning or the end.

REFERENCES

Available upon Request (In today's resumes, this caption is optional or obsolete)

<u>Note</u>: On earlier Resumes, either of these captions: *'Reference available upon request'* or *'References will be furnished upon request'* were mandatory. It alerts human resources to: "*Go ahead and check me out—I have nothing to hide!*" However, on today's Resumes, not only is it optional; in some cases, it is obsolete. This does not mean that references are ruled out altogether. Based on the onset of so many fraudulent/criminal activities, employers are even more vigilant in checking job references prior to hiring a candidate. So, always have your lists of references handy (at least 3 individuals who will vouch for you). You can have this info on flashcards) or create your own—and don't forget to contact the individuals whose names you plan to use before using them—employers do check and listen keenly for inconsistencies!!!

Tips on the Interview Process

After your *job-winning resume* is posted and you are selected as the candidate, your next step is the interview process. Below are some practical tips that will, at least, prepare you for the challenge:

1. Get a good night sleep.

2. Eat a balanced breakfast.

3. Dress neatly and appropriately – Ladies, be modest – don't toy with your hair.

4. Don't wear over-powering cologne – some people are allergic.

5. Don't be late for your interview – plan to arrive at least 15-minutes early–and relax.

6. Wait to be seated.

7. Be polite -- don't chew gum during the interview process.

8. Answer questions promptly and honestly.

9. You can politely decline to answer questions that are irrelevant.

10. Be prepared - take along your list of references.

11. Don't forget to thank the interviewer.

A word of advice to the candidates applying for an executive position:

Once, I had the privilege of speaking to a President who hires executives to fill positions in his company. He said: "Prior to hiring an executive, I would invite him or her out to lunch. When our order is served, if that executive automatically apply salt or pepper before tasting the meal, that person I will not hire." I asked: Why? He replied: "That person is impromptu—and is not solid in decision-making. He or she did not test the water before jumping in." Amazing analogy, with some truth to it. So, executives, be very mindful of this, and don't be caught off-guard!

"To give subtilty to the simple, to the young man knowledge and discretion. A wise man will hear, and will increase learning; and a man of understanding shall attain unto wise counsel."

[The Book of Wisdom: Proverbs 1:4-5]

SECTION FIVE

SAMPLES: RESUMES, LETTERS, REFERENCES

[Chronological Resume]

NAME ▶ADDRESS▶ ⟩▶ E-MAIL

1000 Oak Lane	000.000.0000
Salt Lake City 00000	emailaddress.com

CAREER FOCUS

CORPORATE CONSULTANT…IN A MANAGEMENT-LEVEL OPERATIONS.

PROFESSIONAL PROFILE

Executive Chef, Hospitality, Food & Beverage Director, Kitchen Manager, and Personal Chef qualified by more than 23 years' experience as a *Consulting Gourmet Chef-on-Tour*. Profitably promote and launch new business development consisting of full-service restaurant start-up operations for private clubs, catering firms, lounges and bars across the United States. Traveled globally (on training) to Switzerland, Paris, France, Jamaica and Brenton Woods. Ability to recruit, hire and train staff in *Restaurant/Hotel Management, Culinary Arts, Nutrition, Safety, Food Science, and Technology* roles. Verbal/written communicator; possess strong organization, and problem-resolution skills. At ease in board-level planning and decision-making strategies… Proficiently utilizes modern computer and social media apps.

Core Competencies in:

- Kitchen Operations Efficiency: maximize safety

- Quality Assurance: building integrity

- Budget Planning/Implementation: growing revenue

- Product Development: enhancing profit goals

48

- Menu Planning/Development: strategic marketing

- Policies and Regulatory Procedures: adhering to compliance

- Culinary Management, achieving goals

- Troubleshooting/Multitasking, business growth

- Buffet/Plate Design and Presentation, customer service

- Profit & Loss, Inventory/Control, waste reduction

- Coordinating/Catering Special Events: team-player

EXPERIENCE

Food & Beverage Consultant/Executive Chef/Kitchen Manager   2000 to present

GOURMET CHEF-ON-TOUR, Davie, FL

Report directly to the Corporate Manager, with full accountability to orchestrate and manage multiple tasks through daily consultation with recurring business clients, including the University of Miami, Port of Miami, and Miami-Dade County. Train and oversee internal/external staff to ensure overall smooth operations.

- Successfully launch and open a total of 4 new franchises within the first two years of operation

- Handle budgeting, food costs, inventory and quality control, which significantly increased revenue

- Hire, train, orient and oversee staff of 30, supervising up to a maximum of 100 employees over time

- Conduct feasible negotiations at state and federal levels, in compliance with organizational procedures

- Coach managers in plate presentation, menu planning/ design of service areas for special functions

- Prepare fiscal reports and analyses, identify progress or adverse trends, and make recommendations

Executive Chef   1999 to 2000

VERDI, Naples, FL

Coordinated and managed comprehensive functions as executive chef responsible for purchasing, food and beverages, menu planning, costs analysis, inventory control and employee scheduling for rapidly expanding restaurant operation.

- Designed daily menu and cooked mouth-watering dishes for large scale dining and/or formal occasions

- Chaired weekly meetings to develop managers, Soús Chefs, and front/back of house personnel

- Performed financial and administrative functions, including budget/report preparation and accounting

- Assisted in staff selection, hiring, training and supervising staff to function at peak efficiency

- Troubleshoot and amicably resolved all work-related and guest/service issues

PRIOR POSITIONS

Chef Manager (1995-1999)

ARAMARK, Miami, FL

Designed and implemented sales/marketing strategies to enhance and promote state-of-the-art dining.

Sous Chef (11/1998-1999)

LOEWS HOTEL, South Beach, FL

Instrumental in the timely development and successful launching of Loews brand new luxurious hotel that housed a 330-seat South Beach waterfront restaurant, specializing in American/Argentina Cuisines.

Ella A. Williams

Trainer/Chef *(02/1998-11/1999)*

CHINA GRILL CORP includes TUSCAN STEAK & CHINA GRILL I, Las Olas and Aventura,

Worked closely with coveted Chef's Dewey Lasasso and Robin Hass, assisted from start-up operations to initial opening of fine family-style Ala Carte Dining.

Chef *(11/1997-06/1998)*

Played key role in the overall planning, development and opening of a 600-seat fine dining steak house.

Apprentice *(Apr-Nov 11/1997)*

HOTEL du RHONE, Geneva, Switzerland

Collaborated in six-month apprenticeship in Switzerland with Chef Michele Christol. Relocated to Bretton Woods as a Sous Chef.

First Cook

DORAL RESORT (2/95-9/95), FISHER ISLAND (9/95-2/96), FL

TURNBERRY ISLE RESORT & SPA (11/95-4/97), Aventura, FL

Established and maintained quality assurance and total customer satisfaction in affluent "five star" restaurant.

EDUCATION

Associate of Science Degree in Culinary Arts – The Art Institute of Fort Lauderdale, Florida

[Functional]

NAME ►ADDRESS►)►E-MAIL

1000 Oak Lane	000.000.0000
Salt Lake City 00000	emailaddress.com

ASPIRATION

Securing potential opportunity in which to perform, learn and grow in a novel work environment.

SKILLS SUMMARY

- Objective-driven advancing student currently enrolled in the IB Program at Tucker High School

- Attentive listener/effective communicator with a positive attitude and the ability to amicably resolve issues

- Trustworthy: Possess strong organization, interpersonal and time management capabilities

- Extremely conscientious and responsible; expertise in developing and implementing innovative concepts

- Team Leader/keen adviser with a friendly disposition to interact well with people of all ages

- *Computer savvy in Microsoft Office: Word, Excel, PowerPoint, PDF, Note One and Social Media Apps*

EDUCATION & SCHOLASTIC ACHIEVEMENTS

Honor Graduate – High School Student

- Elected President of FBLA – 2020-2021

- Ranked Third Place in Accounting I at the 2019-2020 Georgia FBLA County Conference (qualified for state)

- Recognized *"Best New Swimmer"* for the 2019-2020 Tucker High School Swim Team
- Competed and qualified at State Level for "*Future Cities 2016-2017 Competition*"
- Principal Award Recipient for consecutively maintaining "*Straight A's*": 2017-2018, 2018-2019, 2019-2020
- Third Place Winner at the 2015 Metro Regional Gymnastics Competition (GGC Gymnastics)
- Participated in the DeKalb County Science Olympiad (2014)

VOLUNTEER/WORK EXPERIENCE

- Provide year-round neighbourhood lawn care and maintenance services

  2018 to present
- Perform weekend babysitting services for families and friends

  2018 to present
- Perform as-needed dog-sitting services for family and friends

  2017 to present
- Participated in Cemetery clean-up with Beta Club

  2019 to 2020
- Facilitated in Habitat for Humanity Build

  November 2019

MEMBERSHIP AFFILIATIONS/HOBBIES

- Vice-President: Future Business Leaders of America (FBLA)

  Culinary Catering: Tucker High School

- Member: National Beta Club

  Chess Club Participant

- Member: Tucker High School Swim Team

  Former Gymnast

- Member: Habitat for Humanity – Tucker High School

  Pianist (4+ years) Genres: Classical/Jazz

Ella A. Williams

[Combination]

NAME ► ADDRESS►) ► EMAIL

1000 Oak Lane   000.000.0000

Salt Lake City 00000   emailaddress.com

CAREER FOCUS

To oversee continuum direct care, preferably in a residential facility that will benefit from the experience and dedication of a diversely accomplished *RN/Health Services Coordinator*.

PROFESSIONAL PROFILE

***Licensed Registered Charge Nurse, Patient Educator, Program Director, Staff Trainer, and Travel*/**Hemodialysis RN with CRRT *distinction. Combined* working knowledge to profitably administrate services in a long-term clinical/non-clinical care facility. Computer savvy in Microsoft Office Suite, PowerPoint and Publisher. Effective communicator with strong organization, negotiation and interpersonal skills to build relations and foster organizational growth. Familiar with daily caregiving procedures and staff control in prior function as Charge Nurse. *Core strengths*:

- Ability to lead Certified Health Care Agencies through successful HIPAA/privacy standard practices

- Full understanding of Medicaid/Medicare protocols and medical/administrative implementation

- Multitask-oriented: programs in compliance with state/ federal and governance of healthcare laws

- Work well independently, or with diverse populations, in delivering superb nursing care

- Conscious in medication administration, intravenously and orally, as it pertains to general medicine, surgeries, transfusion

EDUCATION

Bachelors of Science Degree/Major: Nursing (Dec. 2017) - William Carey University, Hattiesburg, MS

Associates Degree/ Major: Nursing/RN   (May 2007) –

Delgado Community College/Charity School of Nursing, New Orleans, LA

Technical Diploma / Major: Nursing/LPN (July 2002) - Delgado Community College, New Orleans, LA

Associates Degree / Major: Biology, (December 2000) - Delgado Community College, New Orleans, LA

LICENSES/CERTIFICATIONS

• Registered Nurse License

• CPR Certified Instructor • BLS Certified

EMPLOYMENT HISTORY

HEALTHSOURCE GLOBAL, Fremont,   Dec 2016 to present

CHI FRANCISCAN/FRESENIUS KIDNEY CARE, Tacoma, WA

Travel Acute Hemodialysis RN

Work in collaboration with physicians and other healthcare providers, accurately reviewing patient records, assisting in planning and implementing the daily plan of care, and educating patients and their family members on effectively managing related illnesses. Able to and performed Hemodialysis, CRRT, and Peritoneal dialysis independently.

- Assess patients' for pre and post dialysis treatment.

- Initiate and/or terminate dialysis treatment on patients with CVC, AVF, AVG, and CRRT.

- Prepare dialysis equipment and monitor patients for adverse reactions throughout the duration of treatment.

- Records patients' medical information and vital signs.

- Remove femoral sheaths and administer medications, including thrombolytic.

- Monitor inpatient care for irregular dialysis reactions.

- Monitor patients and adjust specialized equipment used on patients.

- Clean and dress permanent and temporary catheters.

- Assign patients to staff while supervising overall day-to-day operations.

- Conduct regularly scheduled staff meetings.

- Participate in hospital management decision-making discussions.

- Administer blood transfusions (all blood products, IV antibiotics and meds if needed).

HEALTHSOURCE GLOBAL STAFFING, Fremont, CA

FACILITY: CHI FRANCISCAN, Tacoma, WA

Travel Hemodialysis RN/Charge Nurse (Dec 2016 – May 2017)

Contracted to assess patients' for pre and post dialysis treatment, developed a plan of nursing care for each treatment, and altered the dialysis management based on standing and current physician's orders.

- Administered meds, and performed computer charting.

- Assisted PCT with initiation and termination of patients with fistulas, cannulation of fistulas or grafts.

- Accompanied MD's on rounds and maintained daily monitoring of the water system.

- Educated patients on ESRD, diet, medication, dialysis treatment, labs and other dialysis modalities.

- Trained and supervised staff nurse and PCTs on a daily basis.

SERVICES UNLIMITED, INC., Shreveport, LA

2016 to May 2017

Registered Nurse/Nurse Educator/Program Director

Worked closely with the clinical supervisor for programmatic guidance to establish and maintain a productive operation system for the administration and supervision of clients' medication and special care needs. Trained staff on the dangers of potential side effects after taking psychotropic drugs, CPR or respite training.

- Coordinated and monitored psychiatric and/or medical care, per physician's order.

- Supervised staff in providing nursing care and services to clients.

- Reviewed all medical treatment orders and implemented new caseloads, as directed.

- Served as a member of the multidisciplinary treatment team.

- Administered medication and observed patients for adverse reactions.

- Worked in compliance with state and federal rules and regulations to minimize error and maximize care.

- Identified and assessed clients for dental and medical needs.

NIGHTINGALE NURSES TRAVEL AGENCY,
Boca Raton, FL   Sept 2015 to May 2016

Acute Dialysis RN/On Call/Charge Nurse

Coordinated and provided care for an assigned group of patients which consisted of assessment, planning, intervention and evaluation for Hemodialysis, CRRT and/or PD diagnosis.

- Assessed patients' response to treatment therapy and made all necessary adjustments to the plan.

- Supervised and monitored **vascular**/peritoneal access care based on procedures.

- Oversaw the delegation of patient care to staff nurses and PCTs, and evaluated technicians on annual performances.

FRESENIUS MEDICAL CARE, New Orleans, LA

Dec 2014 to Sept 2015

Acute Dialysis RN/On Call

Responsible for coordinating care for a specific group, providing assessment, planning, intervention and evaluation for Hemodialysis, CRRT or PD patients.

- Assessed and prioritized emergency situations, and made appropriate medical decisions.

- Supervised and monitored vascular/peritoneal access care in compliance with procedures.

- Instrumental in communicating with medical physicians in planning and implementing plan of care.

- Provided patient/family education, and coordinated daily care with other providers.

DAVITA, New Orleans, LA   **Feb 2014 to Dec 2014**

Acute Dialysis RN/Charge Nurse/On Call

- Assessed patients for pre and post dialysis treatment plans.

- Initiated and terminated dialysis treatment on patients with CVC, AVF, AVG, as well as CRRT.

- Prepared and set-up dialysis equipment, and monitored patients throughout the entire treatment.

- Accurately recorded patients' medical information and vital signs.

- Removed femoral sheaths and administered medications, including thrombolytics.

- Monitored inpatient care for irregular dialysis reactions and adjusted specialized equipment used.

- Cleaned and dressed permanent and temporary catheters.

- Reviewed patients' records with medical physicians helping plan, and carried out the plan of care.

- Provided patient education.

- Assigned patients to staff and supervised RNs, LPNs, and technicians.

- Participated in weekly staff and monthly hospital administration meetings.

- Administered blood transfusions (all blood products, IV antibiotics and meds), as needed.

Ella A. Williams

DAVITA, New Orleans, LA   **Feb 2013 to Feb 2014**

Registered Nurse

Developed, implemented and supervised plan of nursing care for each treatment; altered the dialysis management based on standing and current physician's orders, and assessed patients' for pre and post dialysis treatment.

- Initiated and terminated dialysis treatment on patients with CVC.

- Assisted PCT with initiation and termination of patients with fistulas, cannulation of fistulas or grafts.

- Administered meds and performed computerized charting.

- Attended daily rounds with MDs and monitored the overall water system.

- Provided patient education on ESRD, diet, medication, dialysis treatment, labs and other dialysis modalities.

LSU INTERIM HOSPITAL,
New Orleans, LA   **June 2007 to Feb 2013**

Registered Nurse 3/Charge Nurse

Responsible for and provided overall care to all trauma/surgery patients (GSW, MVC, MVA, Stab wounds, falls), Ortho and medicine patients.

- Administered meds (PO, IM, IV, ID, and SQ), as well as blood transfusions and TPNs.

- Monitored wound care, started IVs, draw blood, transcribed MD orders, and handled other tasks.

- Assigned floor nurses based on acuity of patients.

- Supervised RNs, LPs, CNAs, and administrative clerks.

- Educated patients on disease processes, labs, wound care, medication, equipment, home/hospital and discharge planning.

CHARITY HOSPITAL/MCLNO,
New Orleans, LA   **Dec 2002 to Aug 2005**

Licensed Practical Nurse

Accountable to provide direct patient care under the supervision of an RN Charge Nurse.

- Charted and checked daily assessments performed on patients.

- Monitored blood transfusions and TPNs.

- Administered meds (PO, IM, SQ, and ID) and attended to wound care.

- Rotated on Emergency Surgery overflow unit encompassing Trauma/Surgery/Ortho Medicine.

- Educated patients on disease processes, labs, wound care, medication, and discharge planning.

REFERENCES AVAILABLE UPON REQUEST
[Optional]

Ella A. Williams

[Targeted]

NAME ▶ADDRESS▶) ▶E-MAIL

1000 Oak Lane   000.000.0000

Salt Lake City 00000   emailaddress.com

CAREER FOCUS: ANIMATOR/3-D GENERALIST/ PHOTOGRAPHER, with a passion for Video Games.

EDUCATION

Bachelor of Science Degree in Computer Animation (March 2013) – Full Sail University Orlando, FL

PROFESSIONAL PROFILE

Enthusiastic, deadline-driven, team player—technically savvy in Maya, Photoshop, Python, Z-Brush, Final Cut Pro, Nuke, SoftImage, UDK, Unity, Syntheyes, Endorphin, and Motion Builder Software. Other marketable traits include, but are not limited to:

- Demonstrating a sound understanding in the principles of animation and character anatomy

- Keen awareness in game animation and implementation procedures

- Proactive in motion capture transfer, editing and clean-up

- Troubleshooting: Amicable in problem resolution; work congenially in giving and receiving information

- Receptive verbal/written communicator with strong organization and interpersonal skills to achieve objectives.

ENTREPRENEURIAL/ROTATION EXPERIENCE

KB PHOTOGRAPHY, New Orleans, LA

2012 to present

Freelance Photographer / Videographer / Graphic Designer / Promoter

Independently develop high-quality animations (*Facebook.com/ XDKBP*) utilizing hand graphics and motion data.

- Troubleshoot, organize and accurately resolve technical animation issues

- Implement animations in the graphic editor, and rotate images to launch and/or capture new effects

- Consistently test and maintain animation tools and pipeline articles in the areas of:

  - Modeling   ○ Tracking   ○ Rotoscoping
  - Graphic Design ○ Shading & Lighting ○ Visual Effects
  - Photography

SMILE FOR THE CAMERA, Orlando, FL

2012 to 2013

Freelance Photographer /Promoter

WORK HISTORY

LOWES, New Orleans, LA   June 2013 to present

Paint Associate (Promoted)

Cashier (June to Nov 2013)

- Paint associate providing ultimate customer satisfaction and handling daily cash register sales

Ella A. Williams

- Troubleshoot and resolve service-related issues, working with staff, customers and department heads Significantly increase monthly sales quotas between 15% and 20% through effective time management
- Participate in regularly scheduled staff meetings to keep abreast of organizational growth procedures.

EXCELLENT REFERENCES AVAILABLE UPON REQUEST (Optional)

Guide to Writing Job-Winning Resumes

[CV/Curriculum Vitae: Short Version]

NAME ▶ ADDRESS▶) ▶ E-MAIL

1000 Oak Lane   000.000.0000

Salt Lake City 00000   emailaddress.com

EDUCATION: • **Residency**: July 1999-June 2002

Emergency Medicine

Department of Emergency Medicine

New York Medical College

Metropolitan Hospital Center

New York, New York

• **Internship**: July 1998-June 1999

Internal Medicine

Department of Internal Medicine

New York Medical College

Metropolitan Hospital Center

New York, New York

• **Doctorate of Medicine:** January 1985-
December 1990

Juan N. Corpas School of Medicine

Bogota, Colombia

• **Medical Microbiology Specialization**:
January 1984-December 1984

De Los Andes University

Bogota, Colombia

Ella A. Williams

- **Medical Technology**: 1977-1981
  De Los Andes University
  Bogota, Colombia

CERTIFICATIONS: ECFMG
BLS
ACLS
PALS
ATLS
ABEM

LICENSURE: State of Florida Medical License
Drug Enforcement Administration
(DEA)

**PROFESSIONAL
EXPERIENCE** **Attending Physician, Emergency
Department:** 2018-Present
Mount Sinai Medical Center (FSER)
Hialeah, Florida

**Attending Physician, Emergency
Department:** 2006-2020
Palmetto General Hospital
Hialeah, Florida

**Attending Physician, Emergency
Department:** 2009-2016
Bethesda Memorial Hospital
Boynton Beach, Florida

Attending Physician, Emergency Department: 2003-2006

Memorial Hospital West

Pembroke Pines, Florida

Professor, Clinical Pathology: 1992-1993

De Los Andes University

Bogota, Colombia

Surgical Assistant: 1991-1993

New Clinic

Bogota, Colombia

Medical Intern: 1989-1990

Central Police Hospital

Bogota, Colombia

Instructor of Experimental Surgery: 1988-1989

Juan N. Corpas School of Medicine

Bogota, Colombia

Hematology Assistant Professor: 1979-1984

De Los Andes University

Bogota, Colombia

Ella A. Williams

PROFESSIONAL ORGANIZATIONS

American College of Emergency Physicians

Florida College of Emergency Physicians

MEDICAL RESEARCH

"Relapse following Emergency Treatment for Acute Asthma"

Emergency Department - **Metropolitan Hospital Center**

"Comparison of Continuous versus Intermittent Albuterol Nebulizations in the treatment of Acute Asthma"

Emergency Department - Metropolitan Hospital Center

"Acetaminophen versus Ibuprofen in the treatment of Acute Viral Gastroenteritis"

Emergency Department - Metropolitan Hospital Center

LECTURES

Acute Mesenteric Ischemia

Emergency Department - Metropolitan Hospital Center - August 2001

Thoracic Aortic Dissection

Emergency Department - Metropolitan Hospital Center - March 2000

Complications of Endotracheal Intubation

Emergency Department - Metropolitan Hospital Center - November 1999

LANGUAGES

English/Spanish (fluent: written and spoken)

REFERENCES

Complete portfolio and professional references will be furnished upon request.

Ella A. Williams

NAME ►ADDRESS►)►E-MAIL

1000 Oak Lane	000.000.0000
Salt Lake City 00000	emailaddress.com

ACADEMICA

- *Family Nurse Practitioner Track* at Nova Southeastern University

- Palm Beach Garden, Florida [Spring, 2016]

- *Master's in Clinical Nurse Leader* - Florida Atlantic University, Boca Raton FL

   [Course of Study Completed December 2011, Degree Awarded, May 3, 2012]

- **Bachelor of Science in Nursing, May 2003** - Florida Atlantic University, Boca Raton, FL

- ADN, December 1999 – Bridge Program (LPN/RN) Miami-Dade College, Miami, FL

- LPN, January 1997- Sheridan Vocational School, Hollywood, FL

- Graduate in Health Career Studies, June 1992 - Far Rockaway High School

- High School Graduate, Far Rockaway (Queens), NY

CERTIFICATIONS

Stroke, Triage, HazMat, Trauma Nurse Core Courses (TNCC), BLS, ACLS/PALS, HIV/AIDS, IVIG Infusion, Domestic Violence, Chemo Therapy, Medication Error, PICC Line

Insertion, Cultural Diversity, and Certified Counselor in HIV/AIDS.

PROFESSIONAL EXPERIENCE

Skills-Lab Manager and Adjunct Professor   2012 to present

MIAMI-DADE COLLEGE SCHOOL OF NURSING, Miami, FL

In collaboration with the School of Nursing responsible for the day-to-day operations of the Nursing Skills Lab at the Medical Center, Homestead Campus, and the Baptist on-site nursing programs. Supply and support the needs of students and faculty to ensure the appropriate use of lab utilization disciplines. Develop and implement innovative educational courses via the use of human patient simulators and audio-visual equipment.

- Supervise students in both classroom and clinical settings.

- Facilitate lesson plans and assign grades for classes.

- Comply with all class schedules and deadlines for course expectations.

- Professionally represents the institution in affiliating agencies.

- Participate in departmental and College affairs to provide academic advisement.

- Assist in the development and implementation of course curriculum.

- Recruit nursing students to support the projected demand of the profession.

- Sat on various committees, participating in regularly scheduled meetings and affairs.

Ella A. Williams

- Coordinate and schedule activities among programs that shared space in the Homestead and Medical Center Nursing-Skills Laboratories.

- Made recommendations to Dean, faculty members, and/or Department Chair to implement operational changes that will enhance the Nursing Skills Lab's effectiveness to serve students and faculty better.

- Team with faculty to ensure adequate supervision and use of the laboratory.

- Maintain inventory of equipment and supplies, oversee biomedical for maintenance and repair of equipment, and obtain request for new supplies and equipment.

- Interface with sales representatives, suppliers of equipment and supplies, and biomedical technicians.

- Maintain a balanced budget for all supplies, supervising and acquiring receipt of ordered supplies and equipment.

- Supervise student assistants, tutor, and oversee custodial personnel or others assigned to assist in the laboratory.

- Provide adequate OSHA postings, brochures, equipment and supplies.

- Assure proper disposal of industrial waste, based on College and OSHA standards.

Emergency Department Staff Relief
Registered Nurse/Care Coordinator   2002 to present

MEMORIAL HOSPITAL WEST, Pembroke Pines, FL

Perform onsite triage and clinical assessments in patient care implementations. Serve as patient/family advocate, effectively communicating with physicians, staff, and other healthcare facilities.

- Coordinate and expedite interdisciplinary patients' visits in hospital admission, allocation of services/transfers.

- Comply with Emergency Medical Treatment and Active Labor Act (EMTALA) and CMS Core Measures (CCM) through patient care excellence and proper documentation of treatment information.

- Educate patients on pre and post-procedural requirements.

- Enhance/maintain the facility's MAGNET status through the concept of patient/ family-centered care, embracing Jean Watson's Theory of "Human Caring" in daily practice.

MEMORIAL HOSPITAL PEMBROKE URGENT CARE CENTER,
Pembroke Pines, FL   2011

Staff Relief Registered Nurse

Case Manager - Senior Community Health Nurse 2007 to 2010

BROWARD COUNTY HEALTH DEPARTMENT, Ft. Lauderdale, FL

Worked directly and indirectly with HIV/AIDS patients; successfully linked them with available treatment information and community resources. Educated clients on the dangers of misconception of HIV/AIDS and other sexually transmitted and blood-borne diseases. Mentored staff, Broward County School Board teachers and students, and other healthcare providers in disease prevention by providing integrated support to teenagers, teenage moms, youths and parents.

- Trained, engaged, and oriented teachers, parents and students to participate in school health/education programs.

- Participated in adult outreach and childhood immunization programs and provided family education.

- Collaborated in education and Research Studies with the Broward American Lungs Association along with Broward County School Board to control asthma attacks.

- Measured and audited performance of Broward County School clinics.

Emergency Department Staff Relief Nurse   2003 to 2005

PALMETTO GENERAL (TENET) HOSPITAL, Hialeah, FL

Communicated with physicians and other healthcare disciplines in coordinating and delivering optimal plan of care.

- Provided overall support and compassionate care to patients on emergency and trauma units.

- Triaged, admitted, prepared an appropriate plan of care, and handled discharge procedures.

Staff Relief Emergency Room and
Intensive Care Unit Nurse   2001 to 2003

NURSE PLUS, Miami, FL

Coordinated with peers in planning and implementing top-quality patient service relations.

- Monitored medication administration and pain management processes.

- Educated patients and their families on pre/post care procedures and provided direct patient care.

- Monitored and empathized on treatment for critically-ill individuals to ensure a speedy recovery.

Emergency Room Staff Registered Nurse 2001 to 2002

HIALEAH HOSPITAL (TENET), Hialeah, FL

Charge Nurse: Worked in collaboration with administrators and auxiliary staff in the initiation, delivery, and overall plan of quality healthcare for patients on the emergency unit.

- Educated patients and their families on pre and post-care procedures.

- Facilitated and resolved clinical/medical issues using effective critical thinking skills.

- Followed up on patients' progress and discharge planning.

- Compiled progress notes and documented detailed reports.

Full Time Registered Nurse -
Medical/Surgical Unit 2000 to 2001

BAPTIST HEALTH SYSTEM OF SOUTH FLORIDA/ SOUTH MIAMI HOSPITAL, Coral Gables

Organized and prioritized routine nursing support through assessments, education, planning, evaluation, and implementation of multiple patients (adult and geriatric) on medical/surgical units.

- Educated patients and their families on pre/post-care procedures and provided direct patient care.

- Planned psycho-social needs to accommodate patients in the population being served.

Ella A. Williams

Licensed Practical Nurse/Registered
Nurse – Paediatrics Population   1997 to 2003

PEDIATRIC SERVICES OF AMERICA, Ft. Lauderdale, FL

Provided family-centered nursing support, caring for critically/ chronically-ill children at home and in the hospital.

- Monitored and cared for infants and teenagers who are placed on life support system (ventilators).

- Communicated effectively with interdisciplinary staff to improve the plan of care and provide ultimate satisfaction

PROFESSIONAL SERVICE AND CONSULTATIONS

- Organized/led a successful back-to-school fair for Allapattah Middle School Community, on August 12, 2014.

- Fully support, assist, and coordinate an after school program (CUMBA STEM) at McNichol's Middle School with Global Village Impact Inc., Hollywood, Florida.

- Participate in various Community Services in Miami-Dade and Broward County with Haitian. American Nurse Association (HANA) and Black Nurses Association (BNA).

- CHARP Tower, Miami, Florida, Jan-May, 1999.

- Department of Children & Families, Miami, Florida, Jun-Oct, 1997.

- Sylvester Comprehensive Cancer Center, Miami, Florida, Jan-May, 1993.

- Lawrence Nursing Home, Far Rockaway, New York, 9/90-6/92.

- St. John's Hospital, Far Rockaway, New York, 9/90-6/92.

- Administrated Quality Improvement Services (QI) in reference to Press Ganey and Hospital Consumer Assessment of Healthcare Providers and Systems (HCAHPS) survey systems.

- Compiled document and revise patients' information based on Center for Medicare/Medicaid Services (CMS), providing Core Measure to improve the quality of care within the hospital setting.

- Developed ongoing rapport with physicians, peers and other ancillary staff in support of cultural diversity and to enhance patients/family-centered care.

- Observed and studied the dynamics associated with a cost-effective case management plan.

- Compiled initial assessment consisting of progress reports, allocation of community-based services, and referrals.

MEMBERSHIP & AFFILIATIONS

- Active Member of Haitian American Nurse Association (HANA)

- Active Member of Black Nurses Association (BNA)

- Active Member of Florida School Health Association

- Active Member of Memorial Hospital West Educational Council

- Active Member of Memorial Hospital West Policy and Procedure Council

- Active Member of Emergency Nursing Association

- Active Member Sigma Teta Tau International Upsilon Chi Chapter

PUBLICATION

- Wrote and published Article and Poem on CARING

LANGUAGES & TECHNICAL ABILITIES

- Language proficiency in English, French, and Creole; Conversational in Spanish

- Computer savvy in Electronic Health Records (EHR); Microsoft Office: Word, Excel, PowerPoint, Internet Research, and Social Media Apps

GRANTS AWARDED (Worked on/revised)

- Scholarship from Black Nurses Association

- Foresters Insurance – First Investors Grant Awarded for Back to School Fair

- TD Bank – Community Empowerment Forum

CURRENT RESEARCH INTERESTS

- Nursing Skills Update – Miami Dade College School of Nursing August 2014 and February 2016.

- Involved in research study with Broward County Health Department, American Lungs Association, and Broward County Public School System to Decrease Emergency Room Visits and Increase School Attendance Amongst Elementary Students dealing with Asthma.

HONORS & AWARDS

- Nurse of the Year - Award from Davie Elementary School 6/2009

- Community Service Award 5/2014 – Black Nurses Association

- Honoree by Phi Theta Kappa Honor Society 2014 – Outstanding Educator

COMMUNITY SERVICES

- Homeless Events Global Village Impact, Inc.
- After School Program for Underprivileged Teens (Boys)
- Senior Food Distribution - Fridays (Global Village Impact, Inc.)
- Back-to-School Fair 8/12/2014 – Allapattah Middle School, Miami, FL
- Community Family Dinner Banquet

COURSES TAUGHT

- Community Nursing (Lecture/Lab)
- Medical-Surgical Nursing Clinical
- Medical-Surgical Nursing Skills
- Advanced Medical-Surgical Nursing Clinical
- Fundamental Nursing Skills
- Health Assessment (Lecture/Lab)
- Fundamental Nursing Clinical
- Nursing Skills Remediation

PROFESSIONAL OVERVIEW

- ***Patient Educator/Nurse Practitioner*** qualified by years of experience in providing optimal patient services in specialty areas of primary, secondary, and tertiary care. Extremely accomplished to edify and support colleagues, auxiliary personnel and physicians in Critical Care, Case Management, Utilization Review, and Quality Assurance processes, with emphasis on enhancing organizational growth and achieving operational/bottom-line objectives.

REFERENCES

- Professional references and letters of commendations will be furnished upon request.

SAMPLE LETTERS

[Cover Letters]

JANE DOE

Address	Phone	Email Address

Date

Dear Hiring Manager:

After a rewarding professional tenure in the educational sector, I have elected to start a new career in the Healthcare arena. In this field, I am both passionate and hopeful to make meaningful impact in the delivery of health and wellness. Fittingly, your advertisement for an experienced, take-charge supervisor has sparked my interest tremendously. This is an opportunity for which I am ideally qualified and, as such, have attached my Resume for your review and consideration.

As evidenced in past and present undertakings, I am a results-driven self-starter, and bring to your team a wealth of experience and enthusiasm to assume and handle responsibilities while learning and evolving. In addition, I am relationship-centric and focused in building stronger bonds, as well as planning and implementing evidence-based and trauma-informed practices to enhance growth. Some of my most inherent attributes entail:

- Proactive communication and interpersonal skills: able to identify and meet individual needs across cultural diversity equity lines.

- In-depth knowledge of institutional regulations, policies and procedures that facilitates making more informed decisions.

- Attentive Listening: Diplomatic in amicably resolving issues while establishing and maintaining team morale.

I am a reliable, goal-directed individual, with a strong commitment to succeed, and have attached my credentials as a viable candidate for the position. Please feel free to communicate with me via phone or email.

Sincerely,

Name [Print &Signature]

Attachment: Resume

Ella A. Williams

NAME ► ADDRESS ►) ► E-MAIL

1000 Oak Lane	000.000.0000
Salt Lake City 00000	emailaddress.com

Date

Attn: Human Resources

Re: Name of Applying for

Dear_____:

My interest and qualifications are comparable to the requirements you seek in a candidate to fill the recently advertised position. This is an opportunity in which I can fully employ personal and professional abilities to strengthen relations and achieve bottom-line objectives.

Professionally, I am a proactive team leader, experienced in orchestrating and managing turnkey operations at national and international levels. In addition, I am equally versed in launching new business ventures from the ground up. Under my leadership, third and fourth quarter sales showed steady increase by 50%, organizational goals attained, and revenue growth skyrocketed.

Technically, I am computer savvy, goal-directed and results-driven in training, orienting and supervising staff to function at peak efficiency. Based on these attributes, I present my Resume as a viable candidate for the position.

I am available for a personal interview; please communicate with me at phone number or via email@ _____.com

Thank you for reviewing my credentials.

Sincerely,
Print Name
Sign Name
Attachment: Résumé

[Targeted]

NAME ►ADDRESS►)►E-MAIL

1000 Oak Lane   000.000.0000

Salt Lake City 00000   emailaddress.com

Date

[Recipient Name], [Title]

[Company Name]

[Street Address]

[City, ST ZIP Code] **or**

Attn: Human Resources

Dear_____:

In my quest to utilize well-acquired skills as a passionate, multi-media professional, my research has led me to [name of company]. Located in your neighboring city of Orlando, this presents the ideal opportunity in which I could continue to learn and grow in the intriguing field of Animation Arts. Frankly, I am very enthusiastic in joining your team and have attached my credentials for review and consideration.

Supporting a Bachelor of Science Degree in Computer Animations from New Seals University, Orlando, Florida, are my innate abilities as an ***Animator, 3-D Generalist and Freelance Photographer***. Personally, I am objective-driven, extremely adaptable, and bring to the team a wealth of artistic skills that would enable me to quickly merge into handling various quality production roles. Entrepreneurial experiences have also strengthened my awareness in creating animation state machines and blending art into video game engines. In highestElla A. Williams

addition, I have gained valuable insight in the areas of camera operations, lighting and visual effects, as well as rigging, composing, and animating in graph editor.

Poised, with a willingness to start at any level, I am young and aspiring with fresh perspective to make inroads into modern animation interventions. I can be reached for a personal interview by ꕥ

at _____ or via email at _____ .

Thank you for your time.

Sincerely,

Joseph Doe

Joseph Doe

[Thank You Letter]

NAME ▶ ADDRESS▶ ꙮ ▶ E-MAIL

1000 Oak Lane   000.000.0000

Salt Lake City 00000   emailaddress.com

Date

Inside Address

Name:

Title: Branch Manager

Company/Organization

Address: City/State/Zip

Dear [Name]:

Re: Assistant Manager Position

Thank you for the invitation and opportunity to interview for the above-mentioned position. I left the meeting feeling very enthusiastic about the positive insight you provided me on PNC Bank's operations, as well as a very favorable impression of your overall industry knowledge.

Based on these takeaways, I am confident that I can make significant, comparable contributions to the continued growth and success of PNC Bank.

I am aware that you are still in your decision-making process; however, I look forward to hearing from you again in this regard.

Sincerely,

Jane Doe

Jane Doe

Ella A. Williams

Sample Resignation Letter

NAME ►ADDRESS►)►E-MAIL

1000 Oak Lane   000.000.0000

Salt Lake City 00000   emailaddress.com

Date

Inside Address
Name:
Title: Branch Manager
Company/Organization
Address: City/State/Zip

Dear [Name]:

Please consider this letter appropriate notice and my official resignation from the position as Night Auditor, effective

_____.

Thank you for giving me a great opportunity to work for such a fine establishment. My affiliation with both staff and colleagues, over the years, has been truly rewarding, and I will miss the team atmosphere we have established together.

While it is difficult to say goodbye, I do not rule out the possibility that we may cross paths someday in the distant future.

Again, many thanks for the opportunity.

Sincerely,

Jane Doe

Jane Doe

Guide to Writing Job-Winning Resumes

[Sample]

REFERENCE LIST

NAME ▶ADDRESS▶ ꓕ▶E-MAIL

1000 Oak Lane   000.000.0000

Salt Lake City 00000   emailaddress.com

Ray Jones   000-000-0000   jray25@imail.com

Title: Supervisor

(Company optional)

Mary Jane   000-000-0000   mary5@imail.com

Title: Supervisor

(Company optional)

Jane Doe   000-000-0000   doem5@imail.com

Title: Supervisor

(Company optional)

About the Author

Dubbed a *Gift from God*, Ella is the author of her first book entitled *Guide to Writing Job-Winning Resumes*. This is a journey she achieved through trial and error, sacrifice, and years of hard work and dedication. It is the legacy she vows to share with generations to come. Ella is the President and Founder of SME Business Services (formerly GSL Business Services, Inc.), a successful Secretarial & Resume Writing Business Services in South Florida. A master at her craft, she is passionate in creating and writing job-winning resumes and cover letters, catering to people of all ages and socio-economic backgrounds. For decades, she has served and continues to grow a steady client base of very satisfied customers from different walks of life. Her business affiliations in South Florida awarded her state-wide recognition consisting of a publication in the Miami Herald "Careers & Workplace" Newspaper for her professional Resume Writing style and services, and a spot in the Library of Congress National Register's "Who's Who in Executives and Professionals" for her noteworthy success.

Ella A. Williams, a native of the Caribbean, is also a Naturalized Citizen of Canada and the United States; she initially worked as a Legal Secretary in Canada. An honor graduate from George Brown College, Toronto, Ontario,

Canada, she majored in English Communications and earned an Associate Degree in Legal Secretarial Arts.

An avid Christian and Baptized Faith believer in Jesus Christ; her daily mantra is Psalm 32:8.

Ella continues to remain steadfast in God's glory, motivating, praying and caring deeply for all those with whom she comes in contact, regardless of race, color or ethnicity.

If you found this book useful and would like further help,

I would love to hear from you.

Please email me at

smeinc@hotmail.com

www.ingramcontent.com/pod-product-compliance
Lightning Source LLC
La Vergne TN
LVHW051810080426
835513LV00017B/1888